LABOR PAINS

A MEMOIR

WHEN PAIN MEETS PASSION
TO BIRTH PURPOSE

ASHLEE C. SANDERS

LABOR PAINS
By Ashlee C. Sanders

Foreword by
Min. Latasha Thoms and Min. Latrece Davis

We want to hear from you! Please share your
thoughts about this book with Ashlee by writing
to the mailing address below or by visiting
www.ashleecsanders.com

Published by:
Astounding You Publishing
P.O. Box 19145
Charlotte, NC 28205
Labor Pains: When Pain Meets Passion to Birth
Purpose

ISBN-13: 978-0692693711
ISBN-10: 0692693718

Cover Illustration by Janet Dado
Printed in the United States of America

For purchasing details or to learn more about
Ashlee C. anders and Labor Pains, visit
www.ashleecsanders.com.

For general inquiries/speaking engagements, write
Ashlee C. Sanders at the address listed above or email
info@ashleecsanders.com!

ALSO BY AUTHOR ASHLEE C. SANDERS

30 Days To Make It (A 30 day devotional)

To be released Winter 2016

DEDICATION

This book is dedicated to the Lover of My Soul! My beginning and my end, the author and the finisher of my faith, My Lord and Savior Jesus Christ: Lord, without you, none of this would have been possible. So first and foremost I dedicate this book to YOU!

This book is also dedicated to:

My Grandmother! For always telling me how amazing a writer I was as a child. Those words back then helped to keep me going with this book. I thank you for your prayers that, even after years of you being gone to live with our Heavenly Father, are still being effective in my life today! I love you, and I miss you so much! This… my lady… Is for YOU!

My Children! My "A Team"! My sunshines. My lovebugs. It's been a journey for us, but God has been faithful in His promises. The four of you light up my entire world. You kept Mommy going, even when I wanted to throw in the towel. Ya'll are what makes my life worth living, and I couldn't have chosen a better crew. I truly thank God for my Amaya, Alyssa, Ashton, and Aubrey! I dedicate this book to YOU!

ACKNOWLEDGEMENTS

To all of my spiritual sisters who have prayed for me throughout this journey… I love you all and I truly thank God for your presence in my life.

To My Dumah Darling,

You know it's not often that people come into my life and stay around through the downs of it all. We met with one goal in common, to do the work of the Lord by birthing books to encourage, edify, and uplift His people. You've been my inspiration through this entire process. You've held my hand, you've prayed for me, and never allowed the issues that I've dealt with in this process deter you from being my Sister. You're one in a million! Many have turned their backs, but God has assured me that I have a friend in you and for that I am so grateful! So sister to sister… Author to Author… Here's to much success for the both of us, both individually and collectively! I love you!

To My Spiritual Twin,

I love you love you love you! I promise you there has been no one in my life that could ever replace you. When others turned their backs, you cheered me on. When others laughed, you cried with me and prayed for me! You are the epitome of a true friend and for that I am forever grateful. We nicknamed each other Spiritual Twin and I can truly say that we are alike in so many ways. We have a heart for Gods people, we don't take our positions lightly, and our inner gangsta's are something fierce ;)! I absolutely love you girl and I thank you for loving me and believing in me through it all! Sisters forever! Minister Latasha Thoms!

To My Prayer Warrior,

Your prayers have been so prevalent in my life! There have been many days when I sat alone depressed and feeling so down and all of a sudden, there was a refreshing! So many times, God has shown me and assured me that you had been praying and warring for me in the spirit! I couldn't ask for a different version of you. You're such a breath of fresh air and I love you to life simply because you're YOU! Minister Latrece Davis!

THEREFORE, IF ANYONE IS IN CHRIST, HE IS A NEW CREATION. THE OLD HAS PASSED AWAY; BEHOLD, THE NEW HAS COME.

2 Corinthians 5:17

CONTENTS

Fully convinced that God was able to do what he had promised.

Romans 4:21

FOREWORD BY:

Minister LaTasha Thoms

&

Minister Latrece Davis

In the few years that I have known Ashlee Sanders, I have known her to be a woman of honor, humility, love, and a woman purely after God's own heart. This is a book poured forth from the heart of God. And so I count it an honor and blessing to write this foreward. There is a great wealth of revelation and wisdom to chew on and digest that will greatly feed and impact our spirit. So please don't allow familiarity to breed contempt, but allow the Holy Spirit to be your guide throughout this book.

After being asked to write the foreward for this book, Labor Pains, the Holy Spirit led me to John 16: 21 that says "Whenever a woman is in labor she has pain because her time has come; but when she gives birth to the child, she no longer remembers the anguish because of the joy that a child has been born into the world." There were two things that stuck out to me. One, is that whenever a woman is in labor she has pain. Sometimes we can look at pain in our lives in a negative way. It may not be actual physical pain, but the pain of rejection, the pain of loneliness, the pain of abandonment, or even the pain of being persecuted for the sake of the Gospel. Some pain will have us questioning what we did wrong or even wondering if we are outside the will of God, but that pain may actually be a signaling of something about to break through, or something God is birthing through us. The second thing is that the pain is a revealer that her time has come. Another word for "time" is season. These labor pains are an indication that one season in life is ending and behold, a new season is beginning. The pain may feel intense and the discomfort unbearable to endure, but as Romans 8:18 says "For I consider that the sufferings of this present time are not worthy to be compared with the glory that is to be revealed to us."

Minister Latrece Davis

Normally when we think of labor pains we associate it with babies, doctors, delivery rooms, and things closely related. The labor pains that this phenomenal young lady is about to walk us through is more than just a baby. It's about life, new life. It's about bouncing back from what you were told was going to take you out. Ashlee Sanders in one word: Warrior! The resiliency in this young lady is beyond words. Every single punch life has thrown at her, she has a comeback with even more fight. This book is like none other you have ever read. You will laugh, cry, and may be surprised by her honesty. The world has been her delivery room. God has taken the place of all doctors. Her water has broken. She has pushed. She's had to breathe in and out throughout her journey and now she's delivering this baby.

Congratulations Ashlee! Your baby is precious and will take you through a journey of embarking on so many changes for the good. It's going to blow your mind!

Congratulations reader, you are holding something so precious right now. Allow it to be your wisdom and draw from the strength that Ashlee possesses through God when times get tough. When life knocks you down, this baby will help you to get up. That thing that God has called you to birth out is in you, waiting to be released. Hold on Saints… you're in labor!

Minister Latasha Thoms

To The Woman Like Me...

This book is also dedicated to the woman who suffered. The woman who spent many years not feeling good enough. The woman who rarely felt appreciated. The woman who has spent her life trying to convince others that she is worth it! This book is for that woman who has cried endless tears, tossed and turned, worried herself throughout her days, and felt like she was all alone. This is for the woman who knew there was something more to her life, and refused to stop; no matter how ugly it became. This is for the woman who said enough is enough and who dedicated herself to doing the work. This book is dedicated to me! This book is dedicated to all the 'me's' in the universe. I see you beloved. I've *been* you sis!

Just Breathe….
In through your nose… Out through your mouth…
We've got this!
#ItsPushingTime

Letter To My Sistah's

Hey Sistah,

I'm writing you this letter to encourage you. I'm writing this letter to speak life to you. I'm writing you this letter to assure you. I'm writing you this letter to motivate you. I'm writing you this letter to make you smile. I'm writing you this letter to make your day a little brighter than before. I'm writing you this letter to let you know that… I understand!

In life, it can often times feel like no one understands. Life has its way of doing us in and leaving us out to dry. With life simply happening, it can become a bit overwhelming. Issue after issue, we're left to face the, sometimes grueling, reality of the lives that we've lived. No way to escape the past, so it seems, and every way you turn, there's another issue just waiting to surface.

I've tried, you've tried, and we've tried *so* hard to get it right. Worked our butts off to get one step ahead, only to find ourselves pushed 10 steps back. Discouraged to say the least; irritated to say the most! Life sure has taken its toll on us... Sis, I know!

I remember a time in life when it felt like I just couldn't get it right. I was facing failure after failure, and making one bad decision after another; it was like a never-ending cycle. The vicious cycle of life-Ashlee's version. It was horrible, and I remember wanting out so many times.

What was wrong with me? What was happening to me? Why do I keep ending up here? How did I get here? Oh, and most importantly... Where is God in all of this?

The truth of the matter is, God was there, and is there, all the time. No matter how reckless the decision or how bad the mistake. He never left my side, and I'm writing YOU today to let you know that the same goes for you. No matter how bad it seems at this moment. No matter how shady and sketchy your past has been, know that God is there all the time, waiting patiently for the right time. The time when you'll let Him in and allow Him access to the most secret places of your heart and soul!

As you journey with me through this book, it is my prayer that you relax, open up to what God would have you to receive, and be willing to do the work.

It was in doing the work that I've gained all the things I felt that I lacked in life. It was in the unveiling of the ugliest parts of me and the rendering them unto God that I was liberated and empowered to be exactly who God has called, chosen, and designed me to be!

Take a deep breath beautiful; you've picked up this book for a reason. Now let's get to work!

Love always,
Your Sistah
Ashlee

When a woman is giving birth, she has sorrow because her hour has come, but when she has delivered the baby, she no longer remembers the anguish, for joy that a human being has been born into the world.

John 16:21

TRANSITIONING INTO GREATNESS!

For I know the plans I have for you, declares the LORD,
plans for welfare and not for evil, to give you a future and a hope.

Jeremiah 29:11

Transition: the process or a period of changing from one state or condition to another!

At some point in life, we will all undergo a process we refer to as transition. Whether you're transitioning from renting your home to buying your home, from one position to another in your workplace, from one position to entrepreneurship, or from a hot mess to a messenger and servant of Christ, like me. There are so many different scenarios that could be given that would fall into the category of transitioning.

I've spent a great deal of my life in the process of transition. Lord knows I've wanted it to be over sooner than later, however, there were things that needed to take place and lessons that needed to be learned. While most of those lessons were hard and made me want to throw in the towel at times, they were necessary and vital to the growth process, as well as the birthing process to every spiritual baby that God impregnated me with. So, let's talk...

No matter what you're current state is, I believe that you bought this book because you're expecting something. We don't invest in things to have it lay around the house, at least, I would hope not. So, anyway... You picked up this book, entitled Labor Pains, because you felt like there may be something that you need within the pages. I've got some really great news for you! This book was written with you in mind, and I believe that God is going to speak even louder than He was before to your situation and where you stand in the birthing process.

Right now, where you are, God is most certainly moving things around and causing your babies to leap. You're not imagining things. You're not dreaming too big. You're not ineligible for the things that God has promised you. You most certainly have what it takes, and you can do this.

As you realize and accept that the place that you are in is not where you will stay, God is going to do some amazing things in your life. We cannot be content with our current state and expect for God to place our spiritual babies in our laps. It doesn't happen like that. There's a process that must take place. There are some contractions that must be felt. Whether those contractions are hopelessness, homelessness, abuse, rape, thoughts of suicide, single parenting, loss of loved ones, losing everything, etc. All of these things cause pain in our lives. They come to tear us down and leave us feeling like we can't go on, however, these contractions are necessary in bringing us into the next stage of the labor process, which is imperative to birthing the spiritual babies that God, Himself has given us.

You have to be ok with transition… No matter the pain it brings, just keep in mind that it can't last forever!

A famous singer once said, "You don't have to stay in the state that you're in. The potter wants to put you back together again!" Those words hold so much truth. I remember being in a place of complete turbulence, upset, and chaos. It seemed like everywhere I turned there was an issue to be dealt with. I reached the point of being sick and completely tired. I asked God, how long? How long will I have to endure this pain? How long will I have to go through this mess? What's wrong with me? Why can't I get it right? Needless to say, the answer I received wasn't the detailed answer that I wanted. Lord, I needed you to tell me the date and time that this mess will be over, and all you got for me is, there's greater after this? However, I've come to know that, that answer was more than enough! It was God's promise to me that there is purpose in what I'm going through. There is something at the end of this pain that has my name written all over it and IT IS GOOD!

The fact of the matter is, sometimes life has to tear us apart just so that God can show His Glory by putting us back together again. How could you truly enjoy love, if you've never experienced hate? How can you enjoy victory, if you've never lost? How could you know what it feels like to have joy, if you've never experienced sorrow? Folks that have never been through anything can't speak to the storm of another because they don't even know what a storm feels like.

How could I effectively minister to the hopeless single mother whose significant other just broke her heart, if I never experienced that contraction of heartbreak? How could I tell that homeless family that there's hope and have them believe me, if I never had to sleep in my car with my children? All that we GROW through serves a purpose in our lives, and I need you to know, my sister, your going through it is necessary! Where you are at this moment, in that situation, dealing with that circumstance, you won't be there forever and there is a place called destiny awaiting you. God has you in a place of transition to get you to where He needs you to be. The truth of the matter is, even in the seasons that we feel like we're losing, we win. God allows things to happen to us to get us out of our comfort zones and into His will! The truth in the matter is had He not allowed things to be completely shaken up, we'd still be doing whatever it was that we wanted to do and taking His grace for granted.
The hardest lesson that I've had to learn in life was

how to be a good steward of the things God blessed me with. I've had to lose houses, cars, friends, and family to learn that lesson; although it hurt, I know now it was necessary!

We've got to get to a place of being honest and real and being raw with ourselves. God knows us! We can't hide from Him, so we might as well be upfront and real about our struggles. Don't be ashamed of what you've had to endure. Don't be ashamed of your process. Don't be afraid of what people may say or think, because while there will most certainly be people who are ignorant to what you share, there are still those people who are thirsty to hear you say, I've been there and I've done that, but let me tell you how God did it for me!

In my years of living, I had to make a decision. That decision was, what's more important? Are the faces of men more important than my being obedient to God? Am I more concerned with appeasing people than I am pleasing God? Am I really willing to keep on breaking God's heart just to keep my relationships with man intact? It had been some really rough years leading up to me finally making the decision to say YES LORD and mean it with my whole heart. I had to endure a lot, and I came to understand that until I made that decision with my whole heart, I was going to continue down this downward spiral in life.

I had spent way too many years of my life living for people. I was wrecking my mind, body, and my soul trying to figure out how I could gain the approval of man. These are the same people who told me I couldn't achieve my dreams. They turned out to be the same people who were preying on me. The same people who I called on in my hour of need and they refused to feed me and my children when I was homeless. Yet, I was living to gain their approval.

There comes a time in life when we have to allow God complete access to our lives. We've got to grant Him access to every ugly part of us; the parts that we don't feel so good about, the parts that we cringe at. The parts that we wouldn't dare share with people. It's vital.

God wants to take us from Glory to Glory! He's got amazing plans for us, but we won't experience them until we're ok with being placed into transition. Fighting it isn't going to make it go away. Not acknowledging it won't make it disappear either.
I remember being in school on exam day. My nerves were always a wreck on exam day, even on the days I knew I would ace it. The teacher would go around placing the exam paper face down on our desk and

27

instruct us not to flip it over until it was time to start the exam. He would go over a few instructions and give us the "no cheating lecture" and then tell us to go ahead and take the test!

Obviously, you've got to turn the paper over and take the test in order to get a grade for it. But what happens if you don't turn the paper over? Does it mean you didn't take the test? Does that mean that you don't have to worry about it? No, it means you get a big fat zero on your paper!

Well, when it comes to God, you've got to be willing to turn over the page, take the test, and move forward. God is calling us into a higher dimension. He's calling us into a new place in Him. We can't stay where we are. You cannot afford to stay there! You've got to get up and get going. There are people waiting for you and the baby that God placed in your belly. This process hasn't just been for you, but for those who are awaiting your voice, your testimony, your story of deliverance. Get up, pick up your cross, and WALK!

Are you ready for your spiritual epidural?

As God has placed you, or is placing you, into this phase of transition, I need you to know that it is necessary. It may get intense at times. It will be hard. You may want to throw in the towel, but don't lose focus beloved. God has made you some big promises that He always intended to keep. Here's what He has to say about YOU!

For I know the thoughts that I think toward you, saith the Lord, thoughts of peace, and not of evil, to give you an expected end. Jeremiah 29:11

God thinks highly of you! He knows your worth, even when you don't. He knew you even before He formed you in the belly of your mother! He had plans for you even before you entered into this world. Doesn't it feel amazing to know that even when chaos surrounds you and there's tension on every side, God is thinking peaceful thoughts of you and He has His eyes on your expected end, not on the mess that you're in right now!

As you commit to doing the work and allowing God full reign over your lives, this is my prayer...

Father God,

As you take us from the place that we're in and shift us into what you've called us to be, touch our hearts Lord, and equip us for the journey that lies ahead. Lord, we've been through some things in life that didn't feel so good and we admit we've thought of throwing in the towel on many occasions, but God, we want what you have for us and we desire to live out your will. We've been wallowing long enough, and we've been hurting long enough. We're ready to taste and see the manifestation of your promises in our lives. Help us to become unstuck. Lord, we give you complete access to our hearts. To the ugliest parts of us knowing that you can handle it better than we can. So, as we open up our hearts and prepare for the transition at hand, Lord, we look forward to coming out on the winning side. Your Word promises that we win, and so we shall. You promised to vindicate us, and so, Lord, we trust you. As we commit to doing the work, Lord, we also commit to allowing you to work in and through us! We're all out of fight, and we surrender it all unto you, Father God, and so we consider it done!

In The Name Of Jesus!
Amen!

You Can Do This

I can do all things through Christ which strengtheneth me.

Phillipians 4:13

I remember going into labor when I was pregnant with my oldest daughter. I remember getting up to go to the bathroom at 5am, and that's when it all began. These spurts of pain would hit me periodically, and I'd just breathe through it for a moment, and then the pain would go away. So, I would repeat my breathing technique each time the pain returned because it worked. I'm sure you know that these spurts of pain were contractions, and indicated that I was going into labor. As I breathed in and out, it allowed my body to relax, but there came a time that breathing in and out wasn't enough. What happens when what you've been doing to stop the pain and the issues of life no longer works?

I got up that morning, and got showered and dressed for church, and we were on our way to Sunday service. Still breathing in and out as the pain hit me and then gradually went away. My cousin pulled up to the door, and although it took me a few extra seconds to get out the car, I did it! I enjoyed church that morning, but the pains were becoming intense. Just breathing in and out was no longer working for me, so I would breathe in and out and clinch my teeth together to keep from making any noise. Thank God, that got me through service.

Many woman would have been running to the

hospital by the time service was over, in fact many would have been there 5am that morning when it all started. However, this needed to be the process that I took, and although I didn't realize back then how much this would mean today; MY GOD, I understand it more clearly than ever before!

After service, my mother had a meeting for her Women's Ministry and I joined her. Sitting in the room with one of my friends and her sister while the older ladies met in the other room. There was a pain unlike anything I had felt from the beginning of this process. It was sharp. It was tight. It sent a vibration through my entire body, and breathing in and out while clinching my teeth together wasn't working anymore, and I had to change up my technique again. After trying a few different things, I realized that a CHANGE OF POSITION would alleviate the pain! So, I would stand up if it hit me while I was sitting, and I would sit if it hit me while I was standing. It worked! I wasn't quite ready to go to the hospital, and vowed to go as long as I possibly could at home.

By the time we reached home that evening, I knew it wouldn't be long before I would have to give in and go to the hospital; unfortunately there were no doctors in the house to assist me in this process. I was dreading going into the hospital, and if I had even the slightest clue of how to conduct a self-delivery, oh I would have!

I enjoyed a bowl of spaghetti and hopped in the shower. By the time my shower was over, I was in unbearable pain and the tears were falling something serious!

Standing in my mom's doorway, "Mom, I'm definitely in labor and have been all day… It's time to go to the hospital!"

I walked in my room, grabbed my hospital bag, and I was ready to go at that point! My mom looked at me and said, "Ashlee, you are not in labor, trust me, you'd be carrying on a lot worse than that!" She refused to take me to the hospital, and told me to call the ambulance if I insisted on going and she would come pick me up when they discharged me. She couldn't be serious, right? She was seriously convinced that I wasn't in labor!

That ambulance ride was the bumpiest ride of my life. I don't know if I was crying more because of the pain or the fact that my mother really left me no option but to call an ambulance to get to the hospital IN LABOR!

I was 6 centimeters dilated when I arrived at the hospital. Nurses running around me like crazy people trying to get me hooked up to all of these machines and stick me for IVs; it was overwhelming to say the least. All I remember screaming was, CALL MY MOM! CALL MY MOM! I CAN'T DO THIS BY MYSELF!

I was completely freaked out, and I needed someone there with me. My mom was at home because she didn't believe me. My daughter's father was incarcerated. My friends were all consumed in their own worlds, so I didn't even bother reaching out to them. My sister, well, she would have been here had my mom believed me!

Screaming and crying my head off, I remember shouting, "I can't do this!" One of my nurses came over and looked me in the eye and said, "Honey, you were made for this! You can do this!" and it was then that I adopted the "I CAN" attitude!

Fortunately, my mother, my sister, and my daughter's grandmother all made it before my princess was born, and we had a waiting room of people waiting to see about us! So this is the story all about how I gave birth to my very first blessing, Miss Amaya!

However, I shared this story with you all because there are some key points that God has given me to live by within this one simple labor and delivery process.

We've got to know what works in order to make it through the process. As I was breathing in and out and the pain became more and more intense, I had to change up my technique. God allowed me to learn the importance of changing up my technique, and completely trading it in for His when it comes to making it through the issues of life. We're not always going to be able to defeat the enemy using the same weapon the same way.

God has also shown me through this labor experience that no matter how hard the pain becomes to deal with, I was created for this and it has to happen!

One of the most prominent lessons that I've learned in the process of delivering my daughter was, even when people don't believe you, when you know what God is saying and you know what is happening, you've got to go anyway, even if that means going alone. When it's all said and done, the ones who didn't believe you and countless others will be surrounding you, and will have no other choice but to support and acknowledge what it is that God called you to!

I'll touch on all of these things throughout the next few chapters, but first, I want to encourage you that no matter what your giant is right now in this moment. No matter what it looks like or how it feels, know that you were created to give birth to the vision that God has given you. He's not just going around handing out visions to people and hoping that they can make it happen. He's given that vision to YOU because He knows that He created you for it. Just like my body was created to carry my babies for months until labor where I would have to push them out into this world. You were created to fulfill the mandate that God has placed upon your life. You, my dear, were made for this!

Do not conform to the pattern of this world, but be transformed by the renewing of your mind. Then you will be able to test and approve what God's will is—his good, pleasing and perfect will.

Romans 12:2

CHANGING UP YOUR TECHNIQUE

For everything there is a season, and a time for every matter under

heaven

Ecclesiastes 3:1

Often times in life, we'll find ourselves trying to remedy an issue that we've used to be able to remedy fairly well. It seems like the same issue, handled the same way, but your technique for dealing with it isn't effective anymore.

I remember lying on the bottom bunk of a domestic violence shelter in Delaware, crying my eyes out. I was mad, upset, broken, and almost bankrupt. With all four of my children on the bunk with me, I had one on my chest, one lying across my legs, and one in each arm. Lord, why do I keep ending up in this same exact place? Not technically the same place, but it was close. It was all too familiar.

For the past few years leading up to me being in that place, my life had taken a trip down this downward spiral, and every time I tried to grab it, it slipped from my grip, and here I was again and again, dealing with the same issues. I was sick and tired of everyone around me who was supposed to love and care for me. I was fed up with church folks, but above all, I was fed up with myself.

I prayed and prayed. I cried out to God, begging Him to save me, to rescue me from people, but Lord rescued me from me as well. For a significant portion of my life, I've dealt with a severe case of paranoia.

So, I spent many of my days feeling like someone was after me, which led me to making decisions that would end up working against me in the long run.

My prayer time was when I was commanded to make some changes. In order to see change, we must do something differently. So, God dealt with me in regards to my issues; dealing with the root of the issue, He instructed me to change up my technique.

There are times in life when we have to revise the technique that we've been using; pick up a different weapon of warfare to go to battle with. The enemy knows exactly what hurts us. He's aware of the people that can get to us the most. He's not ignorant about our soft spots and how he can tempt us. He's well aware, so it's vital for us to be well aware of what our Commander and Chief has equipped us with! The weapons of our warfare are not carnal, and when we think of battle we must know that it's not only with our hands that we defeat the enemy, but also with our spiritual armor.

I've come across so many people, including myself, who just want to please God. We just want to do what God has called us to do, and reap the promises that He has made to us, but it seems like we hit more dead ends than anything else.

When what you use to do no longer works, you must change up your technique! How are you fighting? Are you still just talking? Are you using your sword (The Word of God)? Are you wearing your breastplate of righteousness? God equips us with these things to prepare us for the battle that we must fight and endure in order to be who He has called us to be!

Finally, be strong in the Lord and in the strength of his might. Put on the whole armor of God, that you may be able to stand against the schemes of the devil. For we do not wrestle against flesh and blood, but against the rulers, against the authorities, against the cosmic powers over this present darkness, against the spiritual forces of evil in the heavenly places. Therefore, take up the whole armor of God, that you may be able to withstand in the evil day, and having done all, to stand firm. Stand therefore, having fastened on the belt of truth, and having put on the breastplate of righteousness, And your feet shod with the preparation of the gospel of peace; Above all, taking the shield of faith, wherewith ye shall be able to quench all the fiery darts of the wicked. And take the helmet of salvation, and the sword of the Spirit, which is the Word of God: Praying always with all prayer and supplication in the Spirit, and watching thereunto with all perseverance and supplication for all saints; Ephesians 6:10-18

Change what you are fighting with and you change the outcome which ultimately changes your life!

Often times, when I'm ministering to others, they question why they have to endure so much for so long; my question is, what's in your hands and what's in your mouth? What are you fighting with? God didn't share that life and death are in the power of our own tongues with us because it sounded good. He shared this with us because He wants us to exercise it, and learn to speak those things which are not as though they are. He's given us the ability to speak to a mountain and tell it to move, and as long as we believe, it has to move. These promises God made us require some opening up of our mouths and not just opening it to say whatever we're feeling at the present moment, but opening it to speak about what we KNOW. To speak what God's spoken in regards to us.

A few weeks after being at the shelter, I put an application in for a job with a company that I desired to work for many years. While completing the application online, God spoke into my spirit, "It's yours!" If God said it, well doggonit, I believe it! Within a few days, I had emails from the company asking to set up a phone interview time and an in person interview.

Before either interview, I was at church testifying! Before I even spoke to someone within the company, I was writing them as my employer on rental applications. I was speaking what God spoke to me, and I wasn't just speaking it, I was believing it! I got my dance on in church for my new job and I was making arrangements for childcare. I was doing everything that needed to be done in order for me to start, BEFORE the initial interview! Why? Because, I know what God said, and even when the enemy got busy and I totaled my van, and money was running out and my interview didn't go the way I wanted it to go, I believed God! I started that job 2 weeks later! That's the God we serve!

So my question to you, what is in your mouth and hands? Are you speaking the things that God has spoken to you? Even when things start to look a little crazy, are you standing on the promises of God and calling those things into fruition?

Are your hands producing? Are you fighting with the Word or are you still unsure of yourself? The enemy knows when you aren't sure, and he's not moved by uncertainty and loves it when we operate in a state of "well maybe God is going to do it..." and "this is what the Word says and so I guess I have to just wait for it..." NO! We've got to change our language in order to see and taste the complete manifestation of God's promises IN THIS HOUR!

Father God,

Forgive us for not operating in certainty of what You've said regarding our lives. We know what You've said about us. We know that You have plans for us, and that those plans are good. We know that You didn't create us to go in lack but that you've promised to equip us with everything that we need to carry out the mandate that You've placed on our lives. We know that You are far more than able and willing to do exactly what You promised us that you would do. So Lord, today we vow to shift our language to call forth those things that are not as though they were. We have cancelled our dance appointment with the enemy, and we send him on his way, back to his rightful place. We no longer operate in uncertainty, but instead rise in boldness, knowing that we will win against every situation or circumstance presenting itself in our lives at this moment. We are exchanging our words of uncertainty for words of boldness and declaration. We're filling our hands with praise for what is to come and putting on the whole armor and preparing for battle. We know that as long as You are our source, we'll never be left out to dry, and that Your promises are ever so present in our lives. So we count it as done, in your precious Son, Jesus', name! It is so!

Amen!

To every thing there is a season, and a time to every purpose under the heaven:
A time to be born, and a time to die; a time to plant, and a time to pluck up that which is planted;
A time to kill, and a time to heal; a time to break down, and a time to build up;
A time to weep, and a time to laugh; a time to mourn, and a time to dance;
A time to cast away stones, and a time to gather stones together; a time to embrace, and a time to refrain from embracing;
A time to get, and a time to lose; a time to keep, and a time to cast away;
A time to rend, and a time to sew; a time to keep silence, and a time to speak;
A time to love, and a time to hate; a time of war, and a time of peace.
Ecclesiastes 3:1-8

CHANGING POSITIONS

Be strong and courageous. Do not be afraid or terrified because of them, for the LORD your God goes with you; he will never leave you nor forsake you.

Deuteronomy 31:6

When answering to the call that God placed upon your life, you're not just saying Yes to God, but you are now telling the enemy NO! No, I no longer do what you want me to do. No, you no longer have any say so in my life. .No, you can't have my children. No, you can't have my spouse! Its not enough to just declare YES to God, but you've also got to declare that NO in your spirit and stand flat footed on your decision to live for Christ.

I've struggled for years in my life trying to fulfill my yes to God. When I said yes to God, I meant it with all of my heart. I was determined to make it in this walk. I knew in my soul that God was real, and I set out to share the good news with everyone I knew. I wanted to live right. I wanted to please God. It was genuinely my heart's desire to do life God's way.

However, there have been times in my life when I found myself struggling in sin. I had an amazing group of people connected to me. I was doing some pretty awesome things within the community and Lord knows... I could and would get a prayer through for many of those connected to me. My gifts were ever so present, but I was struggling in darkness.

I had it going on, many would say. I was climbing the

ladder to success and I loved what I was doing. I prayed the walls down, spent hours ministering to others, and life seemed to be on its way to where I needed it to be. Then, something happened…

Some old friends appeared, it was innocent, I thought. Going over her house for a night of girl talk couldn't possibly hurt anything.

Those nights turned into drunken nights at the after hours spot. I found myself in pool halls, flirting with the fellas. Before I knew it, I was on the other side of the United States, literally in California, shacking up with a man that mentally and emotionally abused me. I almost lost my mind!

I was laying in the bed one night, crying my eyes out, Lord, HOW IN THE WORLD DID I GET HERE? What was wrong with me? How did life go from looking so promising to… this?

The truth of the matter is… This was the story of my life. I'd reach these peaks in life where everything looked so good. I was serving God and walking in purpose and suddenly, I look around and my entire life is in shambles all over again!

What I've learned throughout this walk with God is

that there are some things that have to change in order to move forward, you can't stay in the same place and enter into the next place at the same time! You have to do away with the old, and embrace the new! You don't buy a new phone to replace the broken one and still try to use the broken one, right?

When taking on the newness that God promised us when we surrender and say YES to Him, there are some things that we should no longer do, some places we should no longer go, some friends that we'll have to cut off, and some drinks we can no longer consume ;)! Things have got to change!

Don't find yourself in the never ending cycle of, "what just happened?" and "how did I get here?" I can't even count how many times I've found myself in this very same place in life. I was sick to my stomach and full of regret many nights, wishing I had made better decisions. I should have been at Friday night worship instead of the late night turn up! I should have done lunch with my Sistahs instead of my get loose crew. I should have told him no thanks and kept it moving, instead of acting like I was strong enough to fight the temptation!

Sometimes, you have to simply change your stance. Change your position and in most cases… you change your life!

Are the people that you surround yourself with going the same way that you are? Is your environment conducive to what God is calling you to? It's time to take inventory. It's time for a re-evaluation. It's time to make some changes. These changes maybe a little uncomfortable for a moment, but I can assure you that what comes after this painful process is worth far more than your mind can even imagine at this very moment.

God has plans for you! Those plans are good! It's time to trust Him with everything in you, take Him at His word, and receive the blessings He has in store for you!

Father God,

We thank You! We thank You that even in our mishaps in life and after making mistake after mistake, You love us just the same. We thank You that there is nothing that can separate us from Your love and that what You've said about us sustains its validity. We thank You, Father, for loving us through our process and caring enough to chastise us. We thank You for seeing us through every hiccup in life, and for bringing us out even better than we entered in. We thank You Lord, for Your promises and we believe that You can and will do exactly what You said You would. We thank You that even when people laughed at us and made fun of our praise because of our physical state, that You Lord, looked at us with loving eyes and embraced us with open arms, encouraging our hearts to continue the race. We thank You for the chances that You've granted us, and we especially thank You for the chance that stands in front of us at this very moment! The chance to reach up to Heaven and take hold of what You have for us. The chance to live another day and to get it right by You. We thank You, Lord, for seeing the best in us when those around us saw the very worst. It's because of You that we have the strength and the courage to make it through another day. Today, we make the decision to never go back again. To never be the same again. To never break Your heart again. To live our lives to please You, because without You, truly we are but filthy rags. So Lord we just say... Thank You!

Amen!

EVEN WHEN THEY DON'T BELIEVE YOU, GO ANYWAY!

And have mercy on those who doubt

Jude 1:22

As you can imagine, I was beyond frustrated and disappointed that my mother didn't believe me when I told her it was time for me to go to the hospital to give birth to my daughter. How could she look me dead in my face, while I was in tears, and tell me that I wasn't in labor?

Little did I know, that would be the first of many people to doubt me in my lifetime. Even as I set out to follow God's instruction to write this book, there were many who looked at me in doubt that I could or would get it done. I've started many things in life that ended up by the wayside because I allowed not only others doubt to resonate in my life, but even my own.

There came a time when I had grown sick and tired of trying to prove myself to people. I was well into my twenties with no sense of fulfillment. My life was complete chaos and everyone around me, no matter how hard I worked, were negative forces in my life. I spent a great deal of my life at that point just trying to get people to believe in me and see the vision that God had given me.

I spent countless days trying to convince people that I knew God, and that I was qualified for what He called me to. That only resulted in me spending even more countless nights torn apart and in tears, wondering if it was even worth it. They'll never see it, Lord. They'll never understand. I've messed up so much already that people will never really support me. I'm tired of being told to get a grip on reality. I'm tired of being made out to be the crazy one.

The truth of the matter is, no matter how much I messed up in life and no matter how big the mistake, there was nothing and there is nothing that I desire more than to be on one accord with God. The truth of the matter is, my heart was hungry and my soul was thirsty for God and all righteousness. However, my desire to please God was jeopardized in the process of wanting acceptance from people and for PEOPLE to believe in me.

I was tired of feeling rejected. I was tired of tossing and turning at night toying with ideas on how I can get people to understand me. Why don't they get it? This cycle continued year after year until…

I had enough. Continuing through this cycle over and over again, dealing with the same people, and getting the same results was getting old; there was something that needed to be done. There was some work that needed to take place. There were some decisions that needed to be made, and I was ready. I couldn't go another year facing the same things, being stabbed by the knife of rejection, and being suffocated by the doubt of others or myself. I gave up!

I threw in the towel of trying to please people. I was done breaking God's heart by caring more about what people thought than what He commanded me to do. The inconsistency had to stop, and I had to make a decision to stand on God's promises. I'm so glad to know that God's promises for my life are YES and AMEN! Even when people are declaring no… When God is saying YES, that's all we need to be sure in our doing.

How many of you are frustrated and disappointed by people in your life who are looking you straight in your desire to please the Lord? They see how much you care for folks. They see the potential you are trying to tap into. They've witnessed your ability; they've seen you work. They know what you're capable of, but because of your physical state or whatever it may be, they seem to believe that you need to get a grip. They've seen what you're going through and they know that you are qualified. It can be frustrating and discouraging to say the least.

I've got news for you beloved! As long as you care more about what people think of you or how much they do or don't support you, you'll be in bondage to these people. You'll be enslaved to what their expectations are for your life, and you'll never be free to be who God has designed you to be. God created you to be great. He created you to be a world changer. He created you to be powerful. He created you to move mountains. He created you be the tool of access that someone else stands in need of. Unfortunately, not everyone will understand until you drop them and their idea that you can't or shouldn't do it, move past it, and woop there it is, in their faces and they can't deny it. It's time to make them eat their words of doubt. You've been digesting them for years. NO MORE!

I thank God for deliverance. I really thank Him for deliverance from PEOPLE! I'm free from doubters and the naysayers. Not only am I free, but God is bringing about correction to those who told me I couldn't and those who ran out of my life when it got a little hectic. He's doing it! That's a vital part of growing past and pushing through the contractions of life. Sometimes you're going to have to make a conscience decision that, this is bigger than me, and turn it over to God. It's not my job to be chasing people down to tell them that I really can do this. It's not in my job description to prove myself to people. It's not a part of my assignment to focus on what others say about me. However, I am obligated to be obedient to the Lord. It is a part of my mandate to be exactly who God has called me to be, and in my obedience to His will, those very same people will come to know that it's not by my might or by my own power, but by the Spirit of God which dwells inside me!

One thing for sure and two things for certain, every person who walked out of my life, every person who threw in the towel on me, every person who told me to get a grip on reality, and every person who doubted me were very necessary in my process. It all had to happen. It all needed to be said. It all had to bring me to a place of pain. I needed those sleepless nights. I needed those weary days. Without them, I wouldn't be able to enjoy the pure bliss and joy that God has granted me today!

Whose report do you believe? Whose declarations are you holding fast to? Do you care more about what they say or are you more concerned about what God has spoken to you? Aren't you tired of breaking God's heart by living to please others and to make them comfortable?

There's a popular song out today by one of today's Gospel greats, James Fortune, that says:

Let your power fall,
When Your name is called,
Prove the doubters wrong,
You're still mighty and strong,
So fight this battle for me,
And help my unbelief,
So I can tell all my friends,
That You have won again!

That song speaks volumes to my spirit. God is so faithful, and when He placed a mandate on your life, He has absolutely no intention on receiving it back. He said His word would NEVER return to Him void, and that it would be established in the land. Let's pray!

Father God,

We thank You! We thank You for the power that You've given us. We thank You for not growing weary with us in our process, and for affirming Your word for our lives time and time again. Lord, we've been concerned about what others think long enough. We've been held up long enough, and we're more ready than ever before to live out Your will for our lives. We thank You for Your promises concerning us, and even more so for your promise to never leave or forsake us. We thank You, Father, that

You believe in us even when we don't believe in ourselves. We thank You that You are our strength in the most trying of times, and that You equip us with everything that we need to carry out Your vision for our lives. So, Lord, we surrender all unto You on this day, at this very moment, knowing that You, who have begun a great work in us, are faithful to see it unto completion. We thank You that we no longer have to operate in fear of failing, but the knowing that if we just keep You first and follow Your instruction that we win. We win, not in the end, not later, but NOW! We claim the victory right now as we break free from the chains that are holding us bound. We declare that Your will for our lives will be established in the land and we'll no longer operate with the spirit of fear, because we know that we can do all things through Christ Jesus who strengthens us! We thank you in advance, Father, for what's going to transpire in our lives, even now. In Jesus' name we pray, and we count it as done!

Amen!

YOU WERE MADE FOR THIS

For you formed my inward parts; you knitted me together in my mother's womb.

Psalm 139:13

I had been pushing for hours in that delivery room, and my daughter wasn't budging. I was exhausted, the pain was excruciating, and when I screamed out, I CAN'T DO THIS, I meant every word. It was the worst pain I had ever felt in my life, and nobody told me it would last this long, JUST GET THIS BABY OUT OF ME!

I truly thank God for the nurses who were evidently anointed to deal with my kind of crazy, and I'll never forget the one who came over to me and looked me in the eye and said, "You were made for this, and you can do this!" In tears and barely able to breathe, I repeated her words, "I was made for this, I can do this!" I turned into a pro at labor in that moment. It was then that I was able to get a grip, breathe through it, and give birth to a healthy baby girl, and I managed to hang onto my sanity, all at the same time!

Just like God created my body and the bodies of other women to carry a baby for months, leading up to a process in which we'd endure some of the most excruciating pain to be able to deliver that child, He created you for the vision of purpose and promise that He has placed on the inside of you.

When He designed woman, He equipped us with ovaries, a womb, a cervix, eggs, and everything else that is utilized within us to make giving birth possible. He designed the body of woman to be able to endure the process that leads us into motherhood. We were made to give birth to the children that He has blessed us with, and although that pain was a pain that was beyond unpleasant, I thank God for the end result! Four children later, I've discovered the technique that works: believing that I was made for this, and I can do this!

For You formed my inward parts; You knitted me together in my mother's womb. In the 139th Psalm, God shares with us this verse of scripture. He formed us and knitted us together, meaning He took the time and strategy to design us to His liking, and most importantly to be able to carry out the mandate that He placed on our lives even before our mothers had given birth to us.

He's already equipped you to carry the vision, and not just carry it, but birth it. How long have you been walking around with the vision, knowing that you've got it, but unsure about how you can bring it to life? How long have you questioned whether or not you possessed the skills and/or qualifications to get the job done? I want to share something with you that many find very hard to believe.

I'm proof that God uses the most unlikely people to carry out some of the greatest mandates. I'm a living witness that God can, and will, equip you with everything that you need to carry out His will for your life.

While my peers were walking the stage at High School graduation, I was laid up in my boyfriend's bedroom, officially deemed a high school dropout and a coward who made the dumbest decisions to my family.

So here I am, a high school dropout, a single mother who struggled with chronic homelessness for multiple consecutive years, talking about how I'm called by God. Can you imagine the side eyes I got and the "girl, byes" that came my way? All the world knew was this crazy chick keeps popping out all these babies in a world full of chaos. Man oh man do I thank God for Jesus!

I even got to a point where I was concerned that maybe I truly didn't have what it took to be who God desires for me to be. Maybe I should wait until I go back to school and earn my degree. Maybe I should wait until my life is settled. Maybe I do need some institutional or religious backing in order to be who God has been showing me that I am for years. After all, there was no way that people were going to support me after all of the messes that I've gone through in life.

One day, I had to make a decision. Did I believe God or did I not. It was presented to me just like that.

Well, of course I believe God. He's God! So, the work began and since I've done the work, I want to encourage you today. I know so many of my peers who graduated, not only from high school but some even from prestigious Universities, who are living their lives unfulfilled. They've gone into debt to achieve their absolutely amazing goal of obtaining degrees on top of degrees, but they're living lives that don't match up with their dreams and they desire something more.

I say this to show that there is no extended education, letters behind your name, stamp of approval from man, or recognition from any institution on this earth that overpowers the anointing that God grants and the call that He made. God doesn't entrust us to carry out His will based on how many degrees we have or how eloquently we speak. He doesn't go through a list of highly qualified (by man) candidates before He gives the assignment. He's not looking for the person with the sharpest suit or the one with the ability to walk in the highest heel. God is not concerned with these things. He's concerned about whether He can trust you enough to see past what you've been through and carry out His will to bring about a difference here in the land.

If you've gone through all of the contractions of life, homelessness, single parenting, depression, hopelessness, rejection, heartbreak, loss, etc.; and you still call out to Him, you still believe in Him, you haven't lost your praise, you still believe that He is able, and you still have the desire and thirst for Him, believe that you are most certainly qualified and God can and will use you for His glory. It's my story, but it's all for His glory!

He knitted you together while in your mother's womb. He knew that you would have wayward children, and so He knitted in an extra bit of patience. He knew that you would have a relationship that would be designed to suck you dry, so He added in some extra stamina. He already knew that you would be up against some things, so He equipped you with a bit more perseverance. He already knew you would fall more than you would have liked, and so He provided you with a little more endurance.

Nothing that we go through catches God by surprise.

He's our maker. He knows His children, so much so that He took His time to be strategic in our creation.

Every single thing that you need to make it in this life, and to give birth to the vision that God has given you, is already inside you. You just have to tap into it and make a decision to not just say it but believe that you were made for this and because you were made for this, YOU CAN DO THIS!

God is not a man; He could never lie. Everything that He said about you is true. Every place He promised you that you would go, you will. Every blessing that He promised you that you would taste and see, you'll see.

Yes, I doubted at times that I could be the woman that God deemed me to be, even while in my mess. Yes, I had a hard time believing at times that He was going to do it, but the moment I made the decision to rebuke the lies of the enemy and believe God and His promises for my life, everything about and around me shifted.

You were made for this beloved, and everything that you've endured in this life has served a purpose. How could you speak life to that single mother, had you not endured the struggles of being a single mother?

How could you minister to that homeless individual, had you not had to sleep in your car, shelter, and anywhere else but your own home? How could you talk to the anger and hurt of the one who was done wrong by leaders in the church, had you not experienced church hurt yourself?

To everything there is a season. That's good news! You've been through the rough spots and the mess thus far. It's time for you to tap into what's been lying dormant inside of you for so long. It's time to believe exactly what God has said about you! He loves you, and because He loves you, He created you to give birth to greatness! You were made for this! Let's pray!

Father God,

I thank You at this moment, Lord, for loving us so much that You gave us everything that we need to make it in this life, no matter what it looks or how difficult it gets. We can rest assured that we were made for this, and there is nothing that can come our way that we cannot handle. Lord, I thank You for each person who has picked up this book and is partaking in all that You've given me to share with them. I thank You for their breakthrough moments and the blessings that are to follow. I thank You for your strategic design of each individual, so that we can do Your great work here in a land that needs You more than ever before. I thank You for the shifting of the mind right now, in the name of Jesus. I thank You that You are revealing to us, even now, the spiritual super powers that You've equipped us with to make it through the contractions of life. Lord, I thank You for what You're doing in the lives of Your people at this hour. You are so faithful, and so we work all the more to be pleasing unto You. Going and doing without grumbling and complaining, because we know that Your plan for our lives is perfect, and never harm us but will help us prosper and give us hope and a future. So Lord, again we thank You and commit to You, knowing that You are God and that Your word will never return to You void. We are because You said that we are! We count it done in Jesus' name!

Amen!

For you formed my inward parts; you knitted me together in my mother's womb. I praise you, for I am fearfully and wonderfully made. Wonderful are your works; my soul knows it very well. My frame was not hidden from you, when I was being made in secret, intricately woven in the depths of the earth. Your eyes saw my unformed substance; in your book were written, every one of them, the days that were formed for me, when as yet there was none of them.

Psalm 139:13-16

MAKING IT THROUGH
THE CONTRACTIONS OF LIFE

And we know that for those who love God all things work together for good, for those who are called according to his purpose.

Romans 8:28

There were some points in my life when I felt like I just couldn't go on. There were moments when it felt like I was going to die, and I began to believe that I couldn't take another thing, situation, or circumstance that life had to throw my way.

I remember sitting on my mother's couch with my car packed down with everything left that I owned, just watching my kids argue and fuss with one another. I had my one year old crying in the car seat, my 4 year old snatching everything that his sisters picked up, and my 5 and 7 year olds fighting over anything they could. I was mentally, physically, and emotionally drained. My spirit man was in a danger zone, and at that moment I was almost convinced that the psych ward would be my new temporary home. I was in major pain, and to be honest, a getaway didn't sound too bad. I needed to get my life together and figure out how to break these chains that I had been entangled with for years. I was sick of myself! I was sick of falling into the same traps. I was tired of dealing with the same things, and here I am, watching my children slowly but surely become the product of a dysfunctional environment; just like me. This could not be happening. However, it was; right before my eyes.

I've reached many ugly periods in life when I just felt

like I couldn't do it. I remember times when I began to feel like driving my vehicle off of the nearest bridge would make life better for everyone. I remember feeling like no matter what I did, it would never be enough. I remember wondering, "what's the point?" I can recall the sleepless nights, the worry filled days, and the humiliation and ridicule that I endured, but I also remember when God brought my labor story of giving birth to my daughter before me and allowed me to learn a lesson from it. These lessons were simply, contractions of life.

When I looked up the word, contraction, one of the definitions that I read was, the process of becoming smaller. I found that so interesting, and as I took some time to allow God's word to fill me with what He was saying by having me research the definition of this word, my mind was blown, but I felt a sense of relief and I realized that each contraction of life that I've had to deal with: homelessness, being a single mother, rejection, feeling like that black sheep, being talked about, being cheated on, being lied on, etc. All of these things had to happen.

I realize that, as I travel through life, there were some contractions of life that needed to take place to make me smaller in the equation and make God bigger. See, there were many times in my life where I was making my own decisions, relying on my own understanding, and using my own judgment. Doing so only landed me in what felt like a never-ending cycle of being crushed. After falling flat on my face time and time again, I realized that I couldn't do it on my own, and so those contractions were minimizing me. They were making me smaller. They were decreasing me, so that I could fully tap into my morphine drip (God)! I learned that there was nothing that I could do without God. I began to lean less on my own understanding, and instead focused more on acknowledging Him in all my ways, so that He would direct my path. Proverbs 3:5-6.

These painful times in life had to happen Beloved. They had to happen in order to get us to our destiny. Not only were these contractions minimizing me, but they were de-junking me. They served as a detox. They had to happen in order for me to become who God designed me to be from the very beginning.

Psalm 51 tells us that we were born into sin and we were brought forth into iniquity. We spent years on top of years having things instilled in us that were not of God, starting from the day that we were conceived. Things that could not go to the place in which God is taking us, things that we've carried around for what seems to be forever, things that will only do us more harm than good. These things were vital in the process because, not only does it prepare us and afford us the ability to go back to some of those very same places to speak life to those going through but it also allows us the advantage of Philippians 4:12. Knowing how to be content in any and every situation throughout life. Knowing what it is like to be in need and also what it's like to have plenty. What if you never went through some of the harsh situations that you went through? What if Daddy stayed? What if Mommy waited until she was established and could spoil you rotten? What if he never cheated on you, broke your heart, or left you feeling worthless? What if you didn't lose that house or that car and life was peaches and cream all the time? What if you were never left homeless and wondering where your next meal would come from? As crazy as it may sound, these things were necessary. No matter what your contractions of life are and no matter how intense they may or may not be compared to the next person's, know that they serve a purpose. Your job is simply to breathe (pray) in and out. Breathe (worship) in and out. Breathe (Praise) in and out.

There may be some times when you have to add onto your breathing technique and add a shout, or a pacing of the floor, or a falling down prostrate before the

King. Whatever you have to do to get through it, do it! Just remember that everything that you've gone through, and will go through, in life serves a major purpose in your process.

You've got to experience some rain in order to really appreciate the sun shining. You've got to first be hungry to really appreciate a bite to eat. You've got to endure the weeping in the night time seasons of your life in order to wake up and experience the joy!

No matter what it feels like, continuously remind yourself that this has to happen! It's just another contraction that I must breathe through. You got this! Let's pray!

Father God,

I love You today and I come before You today to thank You for the relief that many of Your children have received just from knowing that nothing catches You by surprise. I thank You that no matter what it looks like or feels like, that we have liberty in You. I thank You that we can breathe, pray, worship, and praise our way through each and every contraction in life. I thank You that no matter what comes near us, we can keep our trust and faith in You, knowing that You are our keeper in the weariest of times. I thank

You, Lord, for dispatching your ministering angels to touch the hearts of Your people even now! I thank You that You bring comfort, peace, and an unconditional love to our lives that makes it all worth it! I thank You for what You're doing in the lives of Your children today God, and I give Your name all glory, honor, and praise. In your precious Son, Jesus' name,

Amen!

Have I not commanded you? Be strong and courageous. Do not be frightened, and do not be dismayed, for the Lord your God is with you wherever you go.

Joshua 1:9

The Pain Is In Your Court

For I consider that the sufferings of this present time are not worth comparing with the glory that is to be revealed to us.

Romans 8:18

So, you've been hurt. You've been hit with some of the most exhausting contractions of life that you've ever known. There were times when you just wanted to quit. It didn't feel good, and it darn sure didn't look good.

There were some things done to you that you wouldn't ever even think to do to anyone else. There were some things said about you that hurt you to the core. Yes, Mommy and Daddy failed you. Yes, friends and family have forsaken you. You've been counted out. You've been used, abused, mistreated, etc. All of these things have happened to you.

You've cried yourself to sleep on many nights, and you felt like life would never be right. You've made mistake after mistake. They tricked you. You were most certainly dealt a rough hand, but where do you go from here?

One of the hardest things I had to do in life was the work! The work to deal with the root of the issue and to unmask and deal with even the hideous parts of me! Looking into the spiritual mirror and opening my eyes to the truth was almost devastating. I cried like a baby when I looked at that broken woman in the mirror, covering up her truth with good deeds and kind words. I sobbed looking her in the eye, and I realized that she was dedicating her time to fixing everyone else and their issues while neglecting and/or refusing to deal with her own brokenness and that of her own children. It was one of the most painful experiences that I've ever had, but it allowed me to enter into a place of total surrender to God and make a decision to not allow my pain to go in vain. The pain was in my court. It was up to me what I would do with it.

Would I hold onto it, and drown in my own pity? I mean, I could throw a pity party and just wallow there until I die.

Would I hold onto it and inflict the very same pain that I felt onto others, and give them a taste of what I had to go through? I mean I could just keep the cycle going and allow it to become cancerous.

Or…

Would I take that pain and allow it to be the motivating and driving force behind the execution of my plan to destiny? I could take all the negative energy that I've invested in things that would never repay me and routes that would never be beneficial, and shift into a different direction. I could allow that pain to become my passion, and ultimately catapult me into my purpose, which would carry me on into destiny.

There was something about that third option that really grabbed my attention. I began to thank God for the pain and I made a decision. I made a decision to become one with my pain. I became passionate about it, and my heart desired to bring peace, love, comfort, and joy to those out there just like me, those who were hurt, tormented, and alone.

I decided to love people unconditionally and give chances. I learned to not see people for what the human eye can see, but for the way that God sees them. I began to think about how sufficient God's grace and mercies are for me, and I began to render my own measure of grace and mercy. After all, if God can see past all the mess that I've been, done, seen, said, etc. who am I to hold anything over anyone's head about what they've said or done to me?

So, in realizing that the pain was in my court, I made a decision to live past it. I made a decision to not allow it to keep me stagnant any longer. The truth of the matter was, at that moment, life had been an up and down rollercoaster, full of inconsistency, bad decisions, wrong connections, and me pulling dead weight.

Not only did I make a decision to see the absolute best in other people and view them as God does, I began to see myself for who God says that I am. I began to work on loving myself more.

There was no need for me to feel sorry for myself anymore; I didn't need to wish this wasn't my life. As I set out to do the work, God released more and more of the vision, and the more He released to me, the more I understood that every single thing that I went through had to happen.

He wasn't going to send me to the Nations without a story to tell. He wasn't going to send me to the battered women's shelter without allowing me to be relatable. He wasn't going to allow me to go feed the homeless without me having a testimony of how faithful He is to take care of His children, and He wouldn't send the depressed single mother to me had I not endured the journey of being a single mother to 4 children and dealing with all that it entailed throughout the way.

Everything, and I repeat, EVERYTHING that you've endured throughout life has purpose. While it most certainly came to make you bitter, upset, torn apart, mad, and shattered into a million pieces, God can turn every single thing that the enemy meant for evil and cause it to work for your good. I'm a witness.

There's an old song that says, "and we'll understand it better, by and by!" It is my testimony that no matter how crazy life seems in the current moment, and no matter how jacked up it really may be, if you just hold on a little while longer and be dedicated to enduring until the end, it will all make sense, and not make sense, but it'll make you a better you!

So, the pain is in your court. You call the shots. Will you wallow in what your current state says or will you trust that God has a greater plan in store and this pain that you currently feel is temporary and serves an even greater purpose in what is to come?

Let's Pray!

Father God,

I thank You for the pain! I thank You that not only is this pain necessary, but it makes us better for the work that You've called us to do in the land. It equips us to be able to go before the people that You've called us to and to deal in the genre that You've anointed us for. It enables us to be relatable to those areas in which You'll use us mightily and so God, although it hurts, and although it doesn't look good, we thank You for being with us even throughout the storms that we weather in life. We thank You for being our hiding place in the midst of it all. We'll come out not looking like what we've been through yet more ready than ever before to carry out Your will for our lives in the land. We thank You that everything that the enemy means for evil, You are turning it around for our good. Lord, we thank You in advance for what You're about to do in the lives of Your people and the passion that comes from the painful situations and circumstances that we've endured. In Your precision Son, Jesus' name,

Amen

Beloved, think it not strange concerning the fiery trial which is to try you, as though some strange thing happened unto you:

But rejoice, inasmuch as ye are partakers of Christ's sufferings; that, when his glory shall be revealed, ye may be glad also with exceeding joy.

1 Peter 4:12-13

LET'S TALK SUPPORT TEAM…

Therefore, encourage one another and build one another up, just as you are doing.

1 Thessalonians 5:11

Who's walking this walk with you? Whose hands have you been placing the vision God gave you in? Who are you talking to, releasing your excitement, and even your fears to? Who's rooting for you? Who's praying for you or preying on you, and how do you know the difference?

Some of the many lessons that I've learned throughout this journey are that everything isn't for everybody, you can't trust everybody with what God gave you, and sometimes you may even have to walk alone!

I remember wanting so badly for certain people to be a part of what God was doing in my life. I wanted to pick who played on my team and who didn't. Unfortunately, that wish landed me in some not so great situations, and ultimately lead to me throwing in the towel on so many projects, events, campaigns, etc.

I remember lying in the hospital bed, struggling and completely exhausted from pushing. I didn't think I could muster another push out of me. I had been pushing for hours and she wasn't budging. The nurses that I had around me were so sure that I could do it. I'm glad they were convinced, because I most certainly wasn't.

After taking a break from pushing, one of my nurses came over to me and said, "We're getting this baby out, and we're going to do it without a C-section, I promise!" Within those next few moments, she was over my shoulder, pushing down on my belly, one nurse was handing the doctor the suction to pull baby girl out, and I had nurses surrounding me along with my mother, mother in law (my daughter's grandmother), and sister cheering me on and telling me I could do it.

I had been pushing all night by myself. I was exhausted and completely worn out. After that short break to refuel and reboot, my absolutely amazing support team and I were able to deliver a healthy baby girl!

Had it not been for my nurses believing in my ability to get it done, and even going as far as hopping on the bed and coming over my shoulder to help push, the doctor using the suction to pull, and the ones who stood around me telling me how great job I was doing, and even giving me progress reports such as "OMG, I see the head! She's coming!"… I may have laid in the bed a lot longer feeling defeated and ultimately been wheeled down to the Operating Room for a C-section.

In my spiritual walk, I've come to realize that it's vital to have these kinds of people around me. While I most certainly have had my share of burns due to having the wrong people involved, this lesson has been one of the hardest to deal with. I've always been a people pleaser. I strongly dislike saying no, and I hate to be the disappointer. If it were left up to me, I'd have a team of everybody I know, simply because I dislike leaving people out. If people want to help, why deny them?

Needless to say, that attitude is a thing of the past. I've had folks try to sabotage me and the vision that God gave me. I've had people cancel events, call hotels and cancel contracts, make fake flyers using my photos and then post them with cancelled across it, and many more absurd situations where my yes and willingness to confide in them turned around and smacked me in the face.

Some of these people were people I grew up with. Some were people I've helped along the way. Others were strangers who claimed to be sent from God to help me in the birthing process. I believed in all of these people, but the obvious issue is I neglected to consult with God concerning them. I was so caught up with the vision being so big and needing help that I was open to receiving it from anybody. It sounded good to have an assistant early on in the process. It felt great to say, I have a team. It was great to know that I had people around me, but what good is having people around you if they don't believe in the vision the way that you do? What purpose does it serve to have people around you, if they're secretly working against you? It leads to nothing but chaos, confusion, even more pain, and hurt that could have been avoided by simply consulting with the one who gave you the vision, God!

While, it may have been necessary for you to experience the one bad outcome of walking with the wrong ones, if you move forward, making the same decision to not consult God before placing the vision into the hands of another, you are now making a decision to neglect the baby that God gave you.

As parents, we would never just hand our children over to a complete stranger without running all types of background checks, tours of their homes and/or facilities, asking around town about them, etc. and if you're anything like me, you don't even allow people to get close enough to where they can touch or breathe on your child.

So why aren't we that protective of the spiritual babies that we've labored to give birth to? We've got to be just as particular about who gets close to the vision as we are about who gets close to our sons and daughters!

Lose the people who have no sight of where God is taking you, and who are just on the bus because they have nowhere else to hang out. Get rid of those people who aren't willing to give as much as you do. Fire those people who are simply taking up space in your life and not producing a thing! Then get some folks who are going to jump over your shoulders and say, no ma'am, we're getting this baby out of you. Get some folks who will grab the suction and pull you when you can't do it by yourself. Get some people who are going to cheer you on in your state of feeling exhausted. Some folks who are there saying, Don't give up, I see it all coming to pass, you can't give up now! Get some people who believe just as hard as you did in the beginning when you're feeling down, and who can bring that energy back before you; those people who will be your breath of fresh air.

It's time to lose the dead weight and pick up those that are God ordained, the divine connections you need to get you to where God intends for you to go! It all begins with allowing God to close some doors while opening all the right ones. Why not trust the one who is all knowing to bring about the change that is needed? He created the vision, He created you, He created those that He needs in place to insure that this baby is delivered whole and healthy. Who better to choose your support team than God?

There were some times when I had to simply detach myself from everyone around me and go completely alone, while waiting for the right resources, people, etc. to come along. It wasn't easy, but I tell you one thing for sure and two things for certain, it was worth it and it saved me some headaches.

Let's pray!

Father God,

I first come to You asking for forgiveness for not trusting You to bring forth the right connections and help to bring Your vision to past. We ask that You forgive us for our impatience and lack of consultation with You when it comes to placing what You've given us into the hands of another.

I thank you today for Your child, who has made it this far into this book. I thank You for the change that has come and is to come Father. I thank You, Lord, that You are revealing and exposing in this moment those people that don't belong; those people who shouldn't be trusted with the visions that You've given us. Lord, I thank You for removing the veil from our eyes and allowing us to see clearly. I thank You, Lord, that no matter what we've had to endure thus far concerning the wrong people, that You are giving us another chance and causing all things to become new again. I thank You for the divine connections that You already have for us. I thank You for opening the right doors and for sending us people who are willing to jump over our shoulders and assist us in the pushing process to our destinies. Lord, I thank You that every evil word and wicked scheme that has been spoke or drawn up against us and the vision that You've trusted us with is null and void and returned to sender. We thank You Lord, and consider it done in Your precious Son, Jesus' name!

Amen

THAT BABY LOOKS JUST LIKE…

For by him all things were created, in heaven and on earth, visible and invisible, whether thrones or dominions or rulers or authorities–all things were created through him and for him.

Colossians 1:16

"Omg! She looks just like you," and "OMG! He's a spitting image of his father," these are statements that I hear all the time concerning my children, and I'm sure you've heard it or said it some time or another in your own lifetime. It's simply amazing how strong one's DNA can be at times, creating an entirely new being whom you can look at and identify the parents or relatives are almost instantly.

People are always telling me, "You've got to be a Sanders, you all have the same eyes." This is true; we all have these sleepy yet bright bedroom eyes that give off the most amazing brown glare with the light.

This happens when it comes to our spiritual babies too. I remember when I was just so anxious to live out my purpose for God. I was so excited, and I just wanted the vision to come to pass just as soon as He gave me a glimpse of it. So, God would show me speaking to a crowd of people, and I'd put a website together declaring myself a motivational speaker available for booking. He'd show me coaching people through the storms of life, setting goals, and things along those lines and guess what... I'd go make up business cards and declare myself a life coach available for sessions. The truth of the matter was, I wasn't a bit prepared to be any of that. I needed a motivational speech and a life coach to help me get my life together, so how in the world, or better question, why in the world was I creating these fancy sites and advertising myself for positions that I wasn't the least bit ready to be? Needless to say, these things failed, and the websites were down within a month.

This is not how God operates. God doesn't give you a vision without the proper provision in place to see it through to completion. So, I'm sure people would see me posting my sites and they sat back and thought…how in the world is this child talking about being a life coach when every other day she's posting about something going wrong? That didn't look like God, and so it didn't draw a soul to me.

When God gives you a vision, he also causes provision, and He equips you with every single thing that you need to carry it out. He's not giving you an event to host and calling for you to have to postpone or cancel it. He's not calling for you to start a business and then let it fail within months.

It's so important that we trust God and allow His timetable in our lives to be the one that we follow. When we follow the timetable of God, we can rest assured that what He's given us will flourish and be as beautiful as He revealed to us from the beginning. Excellence is inevitable when you allow God to be the center and focus of what He's called you to.

So, even as I set out to write and publish this book, Labor Pains, I took some time to stand back and ask God some questions. I took some time to get to know the vision in detail, as much as He allowed. I took some time to plan, to be strategic, and most importantly, I made a real investment in it.

When God gives you vision, you can't expect to not have to work and invest to make it happen. God desires for all things to be done in decency and in order. His will is perfect, and so all things that He gives are to be carried out in excellence. How can we make the confession that we serve an excellent God, and then turn around and throw things together that have not even a trace of excellence within them?

When God does something in your life, it will be evident that it was Him. People will look at your business, ministry, brand, etc.; just like you all saw this book and thought, that looks like God. That looks like something I need. That looks blessed. That looks like it's going to be deep. It mimics God, and so now the masses are drawn to it. They're engaged and they're indulging in it. Simply because we didn't take matters into our own hands, we waited on the provision, and followed the timeline from God!

Who will your baby resemble? Who does your

business resemble? How evident is God in your brand and/or ministry? What fruit are you producing? I want to make a declaration over your life today…

I declare and I decree that this baby that you're impregnated with looks just like God! It's attracting the masses, and lives are changing, simply because they've come in contact with it. I declare that things are beginning to line up in Jesus' name, simply because you're revisiting God's will His way, and you're getting back to His timeline. I speak life even to those things already publicized and already launched that you're getting back on track and that baby is beginning to look like God even now and so the people are coming and the souls that have been thirsty are being quenched, simply because they've been in contact with it. I declare that provision is already made for the vision and that you are flowing in the excellence of the excellent God that we serve, and it is so.

Amen

For what can be known about God is plain to them, because God has shown it to them. For his invisible attributes, namely, his eternal power and divine nature, have been clearly perceived, ever since the creation of the world, in the things that have been made. So they are without excuse.

Romans 1:19-20

TAKE CARE OF THAT BABY

Moreover, it is required of stewards that they be found trustworthy.

1 Corinthians 4:2

When God speaks to you and gives you a vision to carry out in the land, He trusts you with it. He's not in the business of handing out visions to people who can't get it done. He entrusted such greatness to you because He knows that He has equipped you to carry it out.

So, you've been in a spiritual war, and you've endured all that you've had to endure to get to the point of seeing the vision manifesting. You've endured the contractions, you've gotten through those trying times, and now your baby is in your hands.

I can remember holding each one of my children in my arms for the very first time! I would kiss their foreheads, and just stare at them in disbelief. As I held them, I made a promise to be the absolute best that I could possibly be for them. I promised to protect them, to nurture them, to love them, and to never give up on them. I went through all of that pain to bring such amazing beings into this world, and I was willing to go through even greater pains to protect them.

I find myself to be the very same way when it comes to the vision that God has for my life. I haven't written this book and gone through all the warfare that came with it to let it be just a book. I endured all that this journey entailed to get this book out and allow it to reach the masses. I endured because I know that there are people near and far who need my story, my way. There's someone who was waiting on Ashlee to birth Labor Pains so that they could get their hands on the encouragement and testimony that they needed to push them into greatness.

So, it wasn't just about writing the book. It wasn't even just about publishing the book, but it was about getting the book out there and doing what it took to get it in the hands of the ones who need it; the ones who have been questioning why I have to go through so much, the ones who are wondering why it has to hurt so badly.

There were some things that I needed to do to make this book count. There was some work that needed to be done even after the book sales were made. I had to continue to take care of and look out for what God had given me to birth.

I wouldn't allow people to get too close to my children when they were born. I wouldn't allow just anyone to hold them, and the same goes for what God is doing in the lives of His people. We can't allow just anyone to put his or her hands on the vision. We can't take just anyone's opinion on what they think it should or shouldn't be. We've got to guard the vision and protect it just like a Mother protects her child.

Not everything that presents itself as an opportunity is an opportunity to be taken. Not everyone who comes to help and assist will be able to. It is so important to discern what's what and who's who when it comes to opening up your arms to allow another to hold what God gave you.

Seek God for all things concerning that which He's entrusted to you. Let's pray!

Father God,

I thank You for gifting us with discernment. I thank You for showing us who and who not to allow to touch and speak on the promises that You've not only made, but manifested in our lives. Lord, I thank You that even now You are causing the wrong ones to step aside and making room for those who are called to assist in the carrying out of Your vision. Lord, I thank You that sabotage is cancelled even before it has a chance to get close. I thank You that every foul word, motive, and intention is null and void even now. I thank You for giving us exactly what we need to care for, protect, and guard our spiritual babies. It's because we trust, depend, and rely on You that we can walk in complete peace, knowing that we are covered by the Blood of The Lamb and that no evil will come near us. So we say thank You and declare that it is so in Jesus' name,

Amen!

And now I am about to go the way of all the earth, and you know in your hearts and souls, all of you, that not one word has failed of all the good things that the LORD your God promised concerning you. All have come to pass for you; not one of them has failed.

Joshua 23:14

IT'S BIRTHING TIME

For we are his workmanship, created in Christ Jesus for good works which God prepared beforehand, that we should walk in them.
Ephesians 2:10

Beloved, I don't care where you are physically located. I'm not concerned about what your current situation is. I make this statement boldly as I declare to you that your storm is calmed, and the rain has brought forth the harvest in which you've been waiting for. I speak to your spirit man, rejuvenation and restoration in Jesus name! It's time to taste and see the manifestations of God's promises to you!

At this very moment, I pray that you take the time to reflect on what God has shown you and revealed to you through your process. I pray that you get back to the excitement and positive energy that you held when you first realized that God has a purpose for your life.

God has such great things in store for you, but you must make a conscious decision that it's time to live life God's way! You've endured your trying times. You've held up through the strongest of winds. You've been able to snap back into place when the trials of life came to break you down. You've been able to keep yourself together, even after falling completely apart. You've been able to make it through things people never thought you would and NOW Beloved, Now is your time to bring forth all that God has called you to in this hour. Now is the time that you get to taste the rewards of your labor!

Your struggle has not been in vain. Your yes to God was taken seriously and so now it's time!

Breathe!

Yes, it's happening for YOU, and YOU deserve every bit of the greatness that now sits at your fingertips! It's yours for the taking!

For you have need of endurance, so that when you have done the will of God you may receive what is promised.

Hebrews 10:36

WHATEVER YOU DO… DON'T GIVE UP!

And let us not grow weary of doing good, for in due season we will reaps if we do not give up.

Galations 6:9

Traveling through this thing called life, I recall when I felt like I couldn't take another step. I remember driving that Kia Sedona and contemplating driving it 100 MPH, just to ensure my demise when I hit the trees that the enemy tried to convince me were a better option. I remember the nights I've cried, wishing that people loved me as much as I loved them. I remember walking around with a smile that looked so genuine to others when I was really dead inside.

I cannot count the days that I felt like pure crap and thought of myself as a disappointment. My good days were far and few, and my bad days were becoming something that I'd grown accustomed to. Nothing ever went my way, and I was always messing something up. I had thoughts of myself that no human being should ever have.

I remember feeling like a bad mother and like my children would end up hating me; that was my biggest fear in life. I wanted to be everything to my babies except for a failure, and all I had been doing was failing!

I remember the nights that I gave up. I was done. I didn't want to do this God thing anymore. It seemed like I had more support and things went smoother when I was in the world and so I was determined to go back. BUT GOD!

The God I serve, the one and only true and living God, the one who sacrificed His son's life for me, the one that promised that all of my dreams would come true, He loved me, even in my slumber. He kissed my forehead with His grace and cuddled me in His mercy. He wouldn't allow me to die in those thoughts. He wouldn't allow me to die with that mindset. He didn't allow that to become my reality, and even when I went astray He extended His hand to me. He is FAITHFUL!

What I've learned in life and through this journey is to be who God has called me to be. There has to be a going through to get through to the breakthrough! I had to endure those unpleasant nights. I had to deal with all of those emotions. and I had to feel defeated at times, simply for God to show His face!

Who would have thought, this woman who has failed more times than she can even keep track of, lost more than many can fathom, high school drop out, single mother of 4, with a hectic and sketchy past would be writing and releasing a book, being booked for speaking engagements, mentoring others, leading consultations for businesses and non-profit organizations, amongst many other things? Who would have thought?

As I got closer to the promise and I could see what was ahead, I became lighter, but my mind began to understand what had been happening in the spirit all along! God was simply preparing me for such a time as this!

I'm free! I'm whole! I'm ready!

So it is my prayer for you, Beloved, that you would continue on in this race. I pray that you tap into the endurance that God has given you to be a winner in the end! I pray that you hang in there, knowing and believing that God is faithful, to finish the work that He has begun in YOU! Whatever you do… Don't give up! There will be glory after this!

THE BEAUTY OF MY PAIN

I had the towel in my hand
Hand lunged back, ready to throw that sucka in
I was tired to say the least
Every time I turned around there was something
When would life get better for me?
When would the light come to the end of this tunnel?
I was homeless
I was broke
I was broken
And most days I didn't know if I was coming or going
Single mother… four kids
Daddy's gone
But I'm suppose to be strong enough to handle this
Man, I wish
I was at the end of my rope
Ready to let go
I loosened my grip
As I allowed the rope to slip
I was ready to jump ship
I stood at the edge
Ready to go
Ready to give it all up
Ready to call it quits
But I'm suppose to be strong enough to deal with this
Man, I wish
Failure after failure

Mistake after mistake
Lord, I'm for real this time
I quit!
Just as I turned to walk away from it all
I could smell the fragrance of roses
But the thorns caught my eye
And although it smelled amazing
In that moment I wanted to die
The tears began to stream
As I fell to my knees
I felt His arms wrap around me
And His love, it showered me
I remembered the dream
The dream that He promised to make a reality
All of these things that I've endured
I was broke
I was broken
And most days I didn't know if I was coming or going
But I sat there
Engulfed in His presence
As He revealed to me
The beauty of my pain
I love
Because I know what it feels like not to be
I give
Because I know what it feels like to lack
I render kind words

Because I know how it feels to be bashed
I speak life
Because I know how it feels to want to die
I'm alive today
Simply because I decided
To see more beauty
Less pain
Less loss
More gain
More trust in God
Less shame
Less doubt
And endurance through all the Labor Pains!
There was beauty in my pain…
There is beauty to your pain

LET IT RAIN

The words came to me as I sat in silence
These were words that told the condition of my heart
These words were straight from the deepest depth of
my soul and right to the ears of Father God
I had been living with a condition
I was weary and I was worn
But these words
As I sang to the melody that the angels played in the
spirit
I became lighter
The burdens seemed to be a bit easier to bear
I discovered that there was power within my
wordship that led me into worship
Man!
These words!
They flowed so well…
These word!
They got me through the night
These words caused God to respond
These simple words…
Let It Rain!

AFTERWORD

I was in a place of utter disappointment. It seemed like the harder I worked, the further out of reach the vision became. I was going on my second year of being homeless, and life was a complete blur.

Sitting in my car before going into the store, a Periscope notification came through. Compelled to tune in, I sat in that car, full of expectancy. He called out my name and began to declare greatness in my life. He declared that I would mother many in the years to come, and the words the Man of God spoke following that changed my world forever… It's just Labor Pains!

I didn't know exactly what God had in store for those words, Labor Pains, at that moment, but it set ablaze to the fire that had been slowly dwindling.

In the next coming days, I had to endure some of the most trying times. I remember becoming so frustrated with life. When was my big break going to come? I almost felt as if the promise was being dangled in my face and I was being tormented by it!

Sitting in front of a house, waiting on a landlord that never showed up, I heard God say, Labor Pains! I sat in that car and cried my eyes out when God said, that's the title for that Best Seller I promised you!

I've sat down to complete this book to get it into your hands so many times before it happened. It took sleepless nights, lots of tears, and much fasting and prayer. It wasn't easy to push this baby out, and it is my testimony that God is the absolute best doula there is. Without Him none of this would be possible.

As God brought before me the experience of giving birth to my oldest daughter, and allowed me to see how it related to my life's journey, my mind was completely blown. I began to realize that this spiritual walk was literally a birthing process, and that it is so important to remember that every situation that comes, every person that walks away, every time you lose, every time you're rejected, every time you have to endure, it's just labor pains; at the end of it all is a beautiful promise!

I pray that as you read this book, you were engulfed by the presence of God. I pray that it took the edge off of any pain that you may be feeling right now in your process, and that you're empowered to keep on going.

It is my prayer that you not give up in the pushing process, but you go on to see the promises of God in your life!

Remember, in through your mouth, out through your nose! Ready or not… This baby is coming!

Ashlee

LETTER TO MY PARENTS

I simply want to say thank you! Thank you for giving me life. Words cannot properly express how grateful I am for the ups and the downs that I've experienced with the both of you. It made me who I am today, and gave me the driving force to never give up and to keep striving no matter how difficult it got.

I worked so hard to hear the words I'm proud of you and I love you. I worked so hard and fell so many times, just trying to make someone proud of me.

Life is tough. I was hit with so many things along the way. There were times when I needed your shoulders and they were out of reach. There were times when I just needed a call to check on me and it never came.

I became angry, bitter, and full of resentment until I realized, it was just another contraction of life. It was just labor pains!

The enemy wanted me to hate you. The enemy wanted me to bash you and throw you under the bus, but God has assured me of your love for me, and the fact that you too had to endure your own labor pains in life. So, I thank you for doing what you knew how to. I thank you for doing what you believed was best. I thank you for allowing me to go through the process that I needed to grow through to reach my destination in life.

Mom, it wasn't an easy road for us. We've said many hurtful things to one another. We've made each other cry. We've pushed each other to the side, and we hurried at times to say goodbye… But I know God to be a healer. Not just a healer of illness, but a healer of brokenness and relationships. I know God to be the mender of broken hearts, and so I believe that He is still at work on our behalves.

I publicly apologize for breaking your heart. I publicly apologize for being so full of rage. I apologize publicly for blaming you for my downfalls and shortcomings.

I love you! Way more than words could ever express, I love you and I mean that with every ounce of my being!

I dedicate this book to you!

Dad, I remember crying myself to sleep just wondering why you didn't love me, and why you didn't want me. I remember feeling like it was because I was fat or maybe because my hair was short. My mind came up with so many different reasons why, and none of them felt good.

I always wanted to know what it felt like to be

Daddy's little girl. I always wondered if would you be back in time to walk me down the aisle on my wedding day.

Even in your absence as a child, I included you in my fairytale endings for life, even though a part of me believed you'd never come back for me.

Words cannot express how happy I am to have you in my life today. Not only are you in my life, but you've made yourself available in the most trying times. You pray for me, you cover me, you guide me, and you now give me the words I longed for as a child... "I love you Ash!" You made it back in time to walk me down the aisle on one of the happiest days of my life that is to come!

I love you!
I dedicate this book to you as well!

To My family!

You all have witnessed the fight and the days of no rest. You've witnessed me run to and fro, trying to figure this thing called life out. You've watched me make mistake after mistake and want to give up on many occasions. You've witnessed my struggle and now, I'm so excited that you all can change the channel!

In the midst of those turbulent times, you all have seen me labor to serve others, minister to the broken and abused, and give everything I had to make others smile even when I was faking my own.

Now, you get to witness the faithfulness of our Lord and Savior, Jesus Christ! He's covered me in those not so favorable days simply to prepare me for such a time as this and I thank all of you who chose to pray for me and encourage me instead of count me out. It means more than you know to have your support as I pursue the things of God!

Thank you with my whole heart for loving me, for praying for me, and for encouraging me at the times when I needed it most! I love you all and I pray God's absolute best for all of your lives!

-Ashlee

It Is Finished

www.ingramcontent.com/pod-product-compliance
Lightning Source LLC
Chambersburg PA
CBHW060444040426
42331CB00044B/2600